THE WORST
BOOK EVER

by Beth Bacon

JASON GRUBE & CORIANTON HALE

Pixel✱Titles

Published by Pixel Titles
www.pixeltitles.com

www.bethbaconauthor.com

PO Box 4649
Rollingbay, WA
98061-0649

Text and Images © 2018 by Beth Bacon.

Created in the United States of America.

I. Author: Bacon, Beth.
II. Illustrators: Grube, Jason and Corianton Hale.
III. Title: The Worst Book Ever.

ISBN-13: 978-0-9994324-5-7; ISBN-10: 0-9994324-5-1

(hardcover)

Categories: 1. Juvenile fiction. 2. Juvenile poetry.

3. School & Education.

Keywords: story time, humorous stories, imagination & play, interactive adventures, meta storybooks, censorship, beginner books, books & libraries, read-aloud, school & education.

BEWARE

I am a

BAAAAAD
BOOK.

BAD BAD BAD BAD
BAD BAD BAD
BAD BAD BAD
BAD
BAD BAD B
BAD
BAD BAD
BAD BAD
BAD BAD
BAD BAD BAD
BAD BAD

BAD **BAD** BAD Bad.

Most bad books look forward to hanging out in the recycling bin,

or slipping down
behind a bookshelf,

or relaxing in cardboard boxes at rummage sales.

You might think I would look forward to a life like that, too.

BUT YOU WOULD BE WRONG.

I'm no ordinary
bad book.

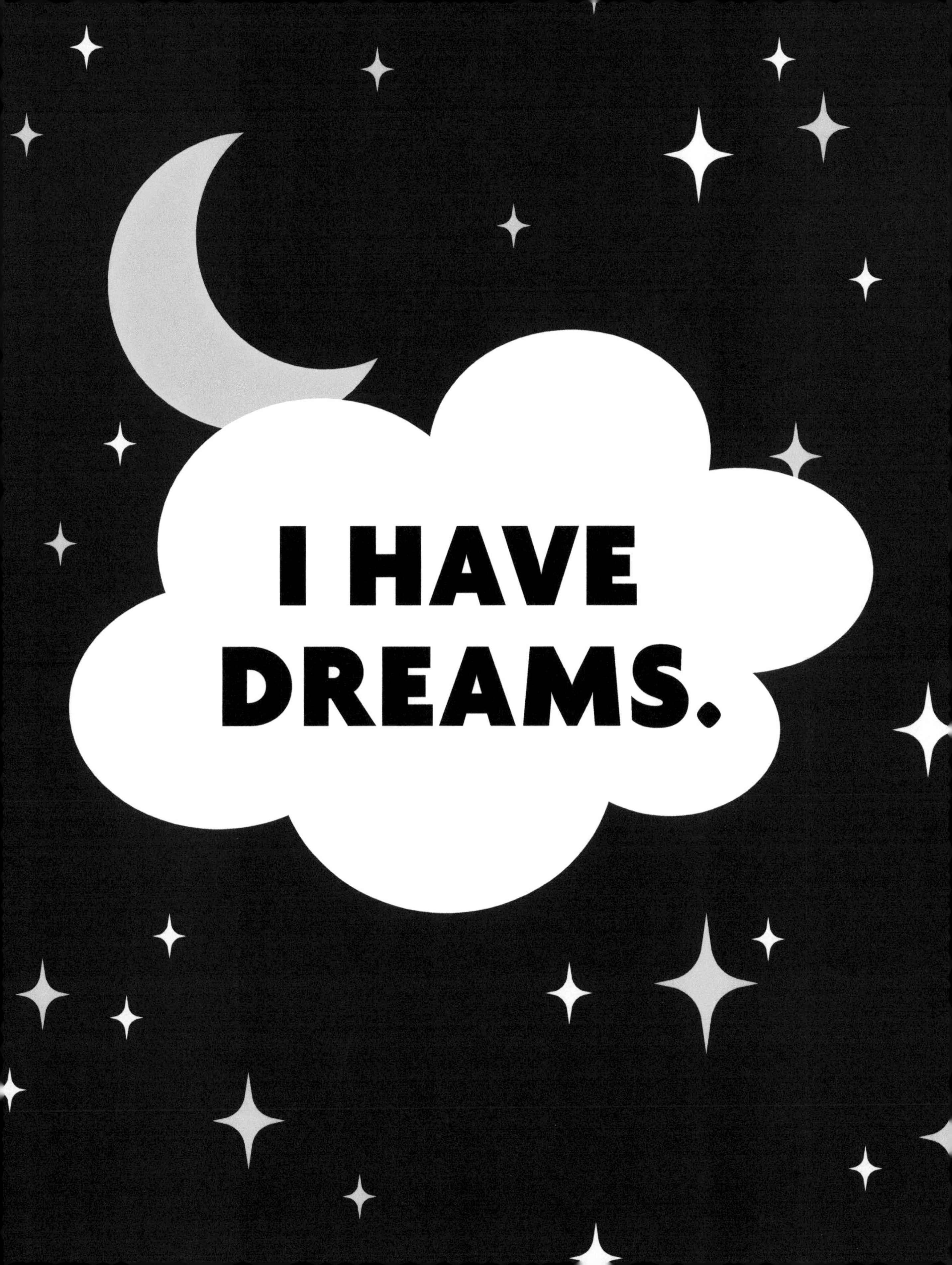

I HAVE DREAMS.

BIG
BAD

dreams.

DREAMS
OF
FAME.

Of notoriety!

Of seeing my
picture on the wall
of a library,

front and center on
the banned books list.

I just have to convince
a librarian to

NOTICE
ME.

So far nothing has worked. I don't know why. I mean, I'm

BAD.

I AM
FULL OF
GROSS
WORDS.

Words like...

BA

RF

BOO

BU

TT

I know, right?
I thought that would
really bug them.

I don't understand
librarians at all.

No big deal. They missed their first chance to ban me but I have a few more ideas up my sleeve.

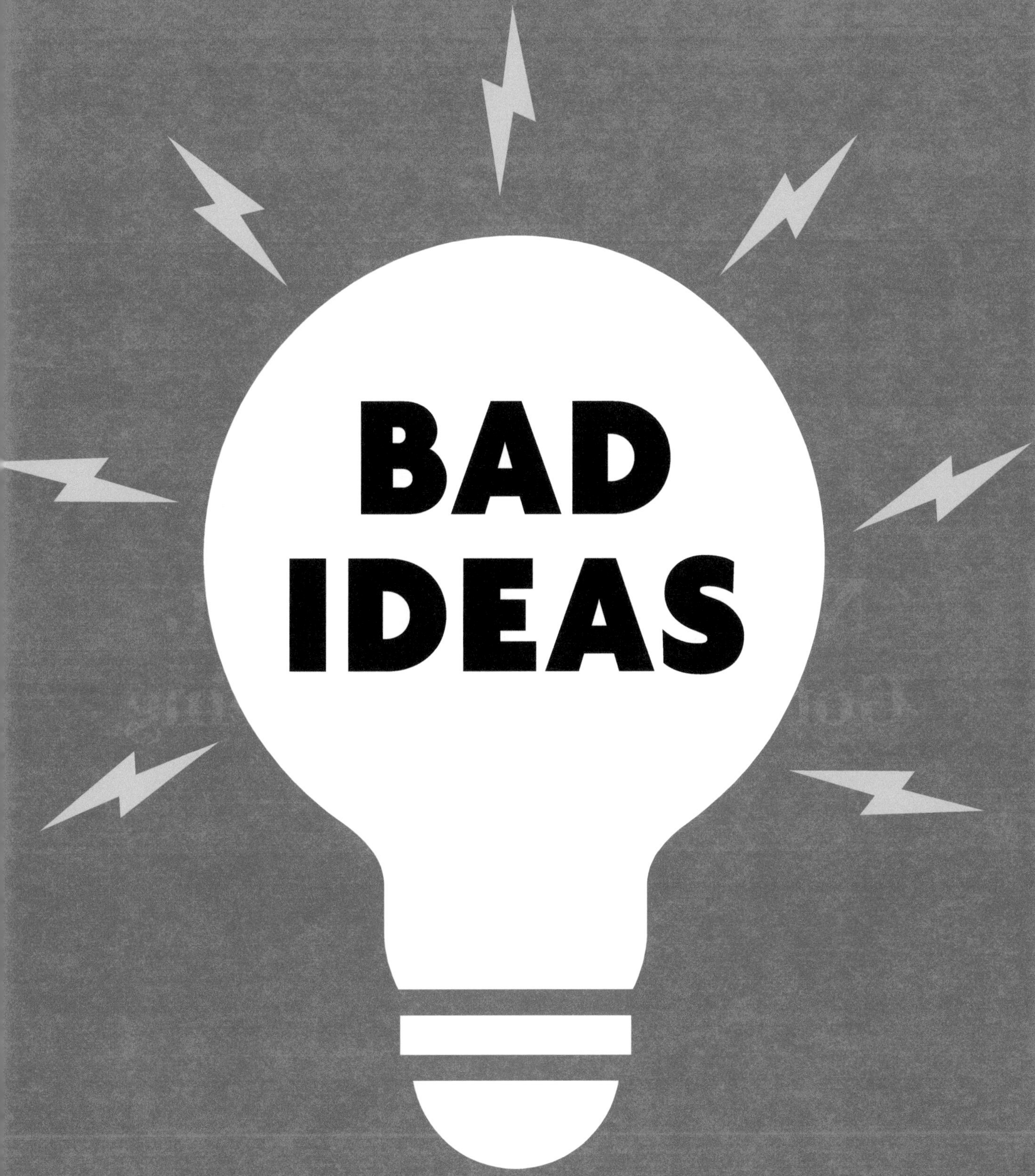
BAD
IDEAS

So leave me alone.
No time for chit chat.
Gotta get to work being

BAD.

I told you,

SKIDA

ADDLE

You're distracting me.

STILL HERE?

You're not leaving?

TOODLE-OO

Adios

BUH-BYE

You're not going anywhere, are you?

GREAT. I'M STUCK WITH A BUNCH OF TAG-ALONGS.

HMM... WAIT A MINUTE.

Maybe you could help me.

Every evil genius needs
some henchmen.
I could add you to my
mastermind plot.

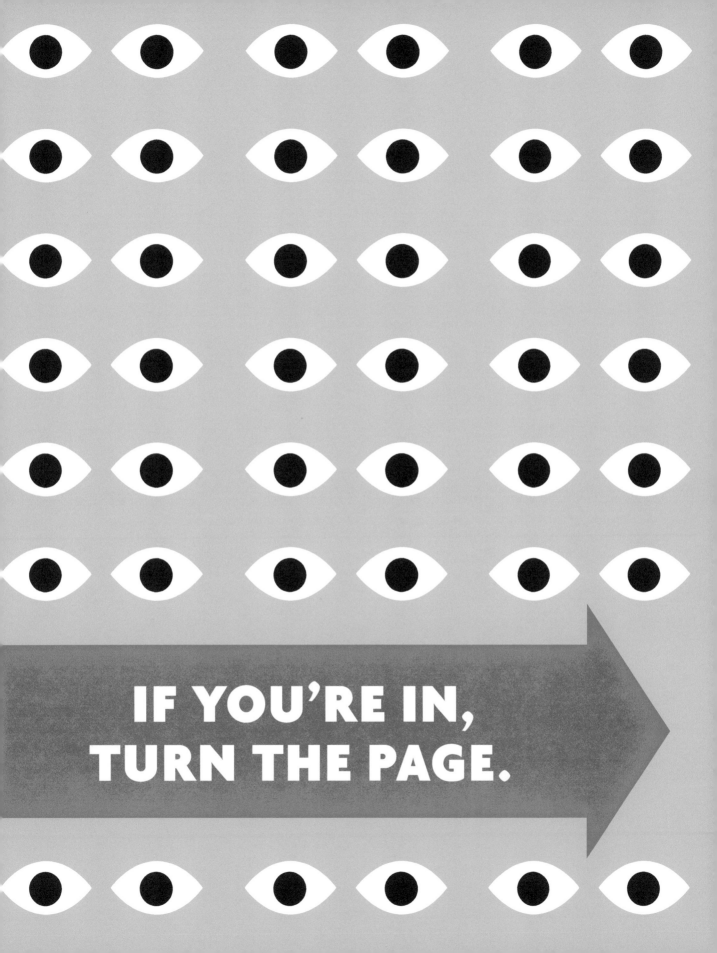

GOOD!

Did I say good? I meant

BAD.

Let's see how bad we can be.

I've heard librarians
don't like noise.
So shout whatever
you see.

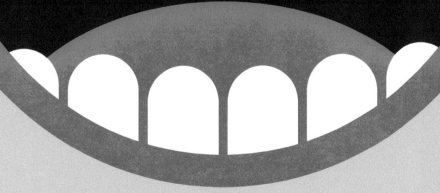

Ready?

You call that loud?

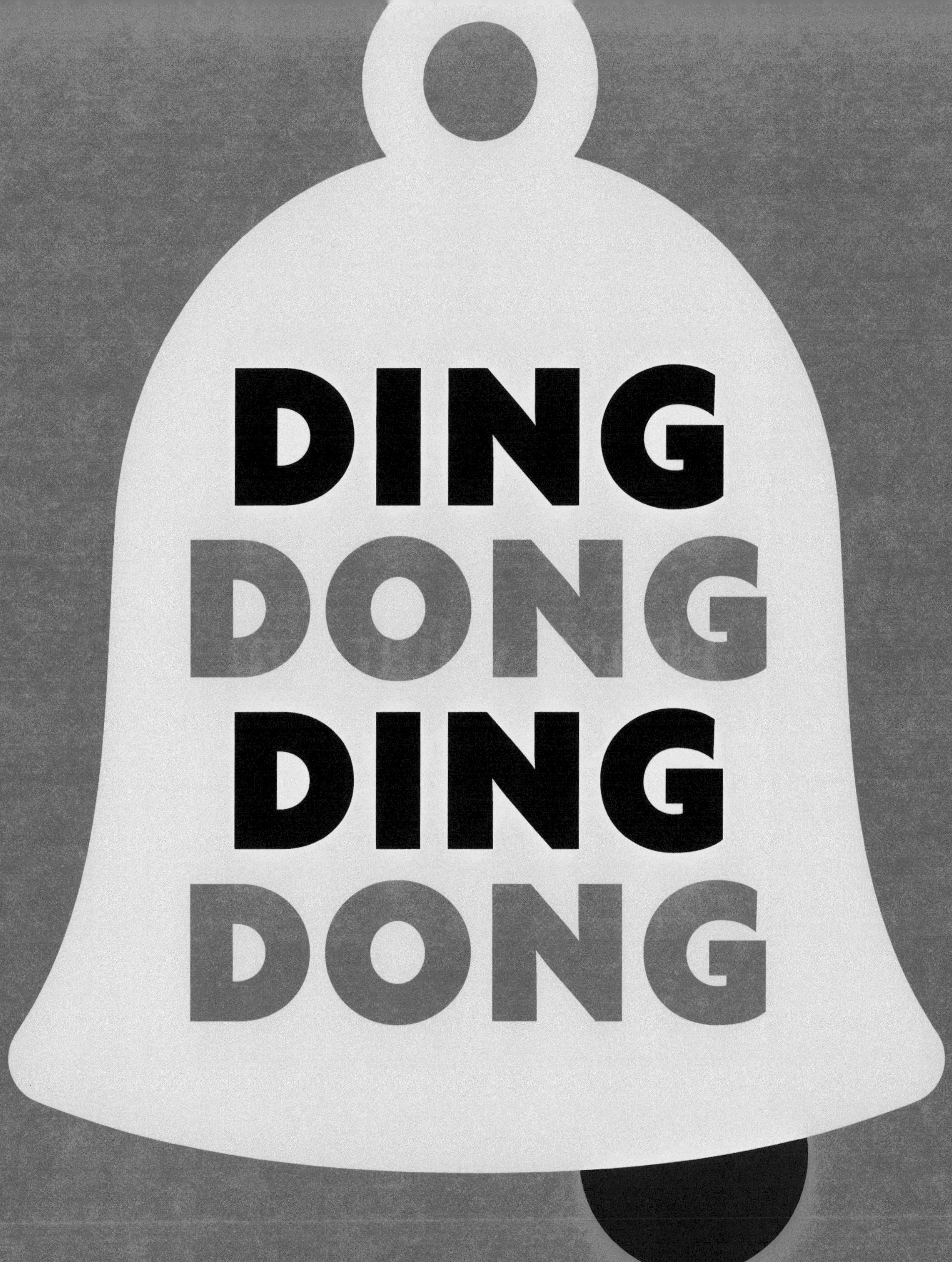
DING
DONG
DING
DONG

That's what I'm talking about.

BOOM!
BOOM!
BOOM!
BOOM!

One more?
Okay.

LA! LA!
LA! LA!
LA! LA!
LA! LA!
LA! LA!

MUSIC TO MY EARS.

Look around.
Any librarians
ready to ban
me forever?

No?
But... But...

WE'RE BEING
SO BAD!

Still not bad enough
I guess.

FINE.

There's worse where
that came from.

Librarians

LOVE

looking up big words in the dictionary.

So I'll make up some words that can't be found in any dictionary.

Flufferfander

flishfoshfiffer

Cobblequacker

quabblecracker

Geggybubber

beppypubber

Now you try.

OH! THAT WAS A GOOD ONE.

I mean a bad one. Not good at all.

That should make more than a few librarians

QUIET
MAD.

I MEAN QUITE MAD.

Not quiet.
Oops.

On teh other hand,
that's brillient! Spelling
mistakes make books
raelly awful.

AND.
PUNCTUATION,
MISTAKES
TOO;

Look around.

Am I banned yet?

NO?

All right.
Time to start moving.

Good books make everyone stay in their seats and stare at the page. But not me.

FLAP YOUR ARMS

LIKE A

CRAZY CHICKEN!

JUMP UP

AND
DOWN

like a frog on
a trampoline.

JIGGLE
ALL OVER

like Jell-O on a
cafeteria tray.

FLAP YOUR ARMS!

JUMP UP AND DOWN!

JIGGLE ALL OVER!

ALL AT THE SAME TIME!

PERFECT

...LY BAD.

Now we can just sit back and watch the banning begin, cause I'm everything

A GOOD
BOOK ISN'T.

And look! A paper! Up there on the library wall! With my picture front and center.

Finally,

WHAT I'VE BEEN DREAMING OF.

What? It's... It's...
An invitation to

STORY
TIME

Story time?

Bad books don't do story time. How could things have gone so

HORRIBLY
WRONG?

1

WAIT ONE MINUTE.

That is me up on
the wall, isn't it?

Looking pretty good,
I must say.

Hmm.

Isn't that what I wanted all along?

STORY TIME, HERE I COME!

AND YOU GET TO COME TOO!

(I couldn't have done it without you.)

It will be the

GROSSEST

LOUDE

MISSPELL

MADE-U

WIGGLIE

ST

ED-I-EST

P-I-EST

ST

story time ever!

WOO-HOO!

We're the baddest. This may be even better than being banned!

WAY
BETTER.

In other words

THE
WORST.

Even so, getting used to all this attention won't be easy for a book as bad as me.

And deep down,
I still hope that
one day I'll be

NED

from a library
somewhere.

The end.

Did you enjoy the time you spent with this book? Please leave a comment at a book review website or at the store where you purchased it.

You may want to check out other books by Beth Bacon.

I Hate Reading
Two brothers offer zany tips on how to avoid their dreaded reading assignment.

The Book No One Wants to Read
A lonely book makes a deal with the reader: You turn my pages and I'll make it fun!

Blank Space
What's your favorite part of a book? One striving reader answers honestly: the blank space!

CPSIA information can be obtained
at www.ICGtesting.com
Printed in the USA
BVHW020906100219
539881BV00012B/61/P